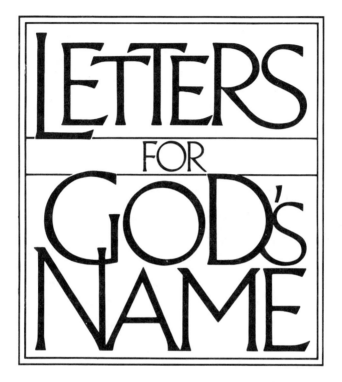

LETTERS FOR GOD'S NAME

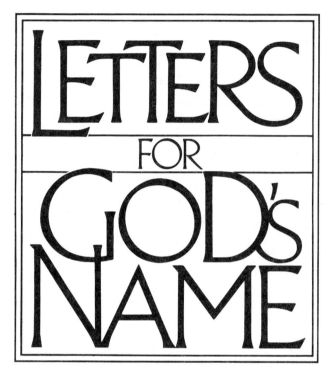

LETTERS FOR GOD'S NAME

GAIL RAMSHAW-SCHMIDT
Illustrated by Tom Goddard

THE SEABURY PRESS

Illustrations: Tom Goddard

Library of Congress Catalog Card Number: 84-51078

ISBN: 0-86683-880-5

Printed in the United States of America

5 4 3 2 1

Winston Press, Inc.
430 Oak Grove
Minneapolis, Minnesota 55403

INTRODUCTION

After one of her divine visions Catherine of Siena wrote, "And what shall I say? I will stutter 'A—A,' because there is nothing else I know how to say." Always we must be searching for words to praise our God, whose name, the Book of Revelation says, no one knows. Always we must be learning to pray: and lest our prayers and our liturgies smother the God they address, always our religious imagination must be quickened. For even our richest and deepest language of faith—the images of the Psalms, the words of the gospel, the symbols of the liturgy—can only hint at the reality of God, and our prayers become poor and flat unless we are able actually to meet God, again and again, in the burning bush, in the wounds of Christ, at the table of the Lamb.

> It is the night of the Passover. A peasant is rushing to finish his work in the fields so he can attend the holy service. But, alas, the sun drops and it is darkness when no travel is permitted. Next day the rabbi spots him and asks him where he's been. "Oh, Rabbi, it was terrible—I was stuck in my fields after dark and had to spend the night there." "Well," says the rabbi, "I suppose you at least recited your prayers." "That's the worst of it, Rabbi, I couldn't remember a single prayer." "Then how did you spend the holy evening?" says the rabbi. "I could only recite the alphabet and pray that God would rearrange the letters."

So we begin again with our ABCs. And we begin together: For even while weeping at the tombstone we never pray alone. God will lead: let's get going. For you, to God, I offer this primer of praise.

Feast of St. Mary Magdalene

Not every woman was born to bear. Some die still girls, and others molder into the grave having borne fruit other than children ripe or rotten. Such perhaps was Anna, old woman in Advent, eighty-four or more, bearing only a word for all who would hear. Grande dame or hag, this prophetess—we do not know. Regal robes or decrepit rags; long white hair, thin and bound in back, or balded by a strange disease which made the children laugh and cringe—we do not know. An early Anselm, a Sophia seeking understanding, or simply senile—we cannot guess. But probably this wise widow, seeing visions, praising God, proclaiming truth, snagging the youth with her raspy ecstasy, probably she had borne no children, or none alive, or none at least to claim her. The temple took her—mother superior, sibyl, or bag lady—and she bore a word of God.

Advent is not only maiden Mary, youth and fecundity and hope. One hears from bolder preachers these days, "Advent is like being pregnant"; God is like bearing healthy children; the word of God is a bouncing boy, as if meeting God were imaged only by a precisely nine-month wait, a day of pain, and then the shared joy of a healthy infant.

Advent, the coming of God, is also Anna, mysterious prophetess of the temple. For meeting God is also like a barren old woman with empty breasts and useless womb who waits not a year to bear a child, but for years unknown, and finally waits for death, to catch sight of someone else's baby and to see in that other life the life of God. Meeting God is like the patient doddering dame, trusting until death that God has indeed come into the world. God's Advent is heralded abroad by the shaky songs of old woman Anna, sharing a cane with old man Simeon, they leaning on each other in the hallways of the courts of the Lord.

It is blasphemous, some religions say, to see almighty God in Advent's womb. But an antidote to the poison of our simplistic Christmas crêches is to see God in Advent's Anna, the old woman waiting: Anna, offering the Messiah, singing of Alpha, fumbling through a rickety dance, infirm joints crackling in the glory of the temple of God.

Before the mountains were brought forth,
or the land and the earth were born,
  from age to age you are God.
The span of our life is seventy years,
perhaps in strength even eighty;
  yet the sum of them is but labor and sorrow,
  for they pass away quickly and we are gone.
Return, O LORD; how long will you tarry?
  be gracious to your servants.
Satisfy us by your loving-kindness in the morning;
  so shall we rejoice and be glad all the days of our
    life.

(Psalm 90)

Many of us are bathed into God as babies.

God as the Bath: the waters holding all earthly life before creation took form; the womb waters, protecting and nurturing the preborn child; the dew with its nascent oxygen, cleaning dirty feet; soothing steam for aching limbs; a cold compress for fevered foreheads; tears to wash dust from the eyes.

(But what is this? Romantic Emerson again, God-is-water and water-is-God? God as a swashing lakeside, God as the salty sea, God as a mountain spring, God as a tub filled with water and kids on Saturday night?)

All I recall from college biology is looking through a microscope at pond water—a supposedly stagnant pool bathing forever innumerable forms of life. Water, water—and so Mark Twain wrote a children's adventure of the River bringing freedom to Huck Finn. Yet Twain set the manuscript aside for some years. And when he finally resumed his writing, the turn up the Ohio had been missed and the River carried Jim toward ever-crueler slavery. Water, for something so common, is a complicated thing, say those who after the flood's devastation rebuild their shacks on the same riverbank. For the water is both their destruction and their lifeline. If God is the Bath, is God also the flood, the waters from which we retreat and the waters within which we flounder?

> *By day and night I cry to you;*
>   *all your great waves overwhelm me.*
>
>   *(Psalm 88)*

The people of God remember many divine baths. Naaman washes in the Jordan and is healed of leprosy. The blind man washes in Siloam's pool and receives his sight. The sea covers the Egyptian army. But that same sea is Leviathan's abode:

> *Save me, O God,*
>   *for the waters have risen up to my neck.*
> *I have come into deep waters,*
>   *and the torrent washes over me.*
>
>   *(Psalm 69)*

As the illustrator Peter Spier showed us, what about all the animals who remained outside, watching the ark as the water climbed up their legs? Paul talks of baptism as a drowning, a bath into death. We who baptize mostly infants are afraid to get the frilly dress wet or think ourselves like a sanctified Dr. Leboyer to float the child into a peaceable kingdom. No, it is more that we hold the catechumens under water, pushing them down three times into the bath, until they burst out gasping, escaping from God's washing into the ordinary life of air. "If I do not wash you, you have no part in me," says Jesus, from whose wounds poured blood and water.

God as the Bath? "The Mystic Bath," by the seventeenth-century artist Jean Bellegambe, depicts Christ high in the air on the cross, flanked by angels, blood streaming from his

4

wounds. But this crucifix is not grounded on Calvary, attended by wailing women. Rather, at the foot of Christ is a golden tub, a great baptismal font, filled with naked dancing people. Several more men are climbing into the pool and a woman, beginning to undress, is unfastening her hair. However, this mystic bath of God, this medieval hot tub, is brimming with blood, the naked Christians washing one another with the blood that pours down from the cross.

It is not only that God is both, the waters of the womb and the water which fills the lungs of the drowning child, a God of life in spite of death. Rather, it is that our God reigns over life through death. Death finally serves the purposes of life, we proclaim at the funeral. Our talk of baptism as the bath which drowns is a way to image God, a God who is the Bath beyond our knowledge of water, a God whose bathings accomplish far more, and other, than simple washings. And so in Narnia, Jill, shaking terrified before Aslan, the great Lion over the whole wood, asks him, "Do you eat girls?" The Lion replies, "I have swallowed up girls and boys, women and men, kings and emperors, cities and realms." For Aslan is not a *tame* Lion.

Daily we bathe in God. We immerse ourselves in the sea of God, overwhelmed by the divine waves, buoyed up again by the undercurrents of God's name.

O God, you are my God; eagerly I seek you;
my soul thirsts for you, my flesh faints for you,
as in a barren and dry land where there is no
    water.

                                              (Psalm 63)

5

In the Seder four cups of wine are raised. The first one sanctifies the feast; the second accompanies the telling of the tale—its volume of wine lessened by ten drops, ten drops given up in sorrow for the sufferings of the Egyptians. The third cup, "the cup of blessing," praises God for the meal and for salvation; and the last cup, to anticipate the end time, cries out, "Next year in Jerusalem!" Historians of liturgy like to see a connection between the Jewish cup of blessing and the Christian cup of eucharist, for at table with the disciples Jesus raised the cup after dinner to bless God for salvation.

But there is yet a fifth cup, the cup of Elijah. It stands filled with wine at a place set for that great harbinger of God, because maybe, just maybe, this year, this Passover, God will come here, to our dinner table, in the divine messenger Elijah. At one point during the Seder ritual the door of the house is opened and the outside steps searched: Was that sound we heard possibly Elijah's knock? No, I can't see Elijah there after all. And sometime during the evening, perhaps as the children are searching for the hidden matzo, the cup gets mysteriously drained, and the children return to table to wonder whether God did, after all, send Elijah that year.

There is a way that we can see Elijah's cup as the one we Christians drain at the eucharistic meal. We can imagine that this holy cup is the one waiting through the ages to delight God's messenger, the draught which heralds the new age. Each eucharist is a celebration of the resurrection, each resurrection a Passover: This cup is reserved for and finally drunk by the one sent by God. It is as if we were sharing a meal of hope, and we opened the door because we thought we heard a knock; or perhaps the doors were locked for fear, and suddenly God has sent One to be at table with us. By this new Elijah the meal is sanctified as never before. God is present, and the meal has been transformed into a time of wonder. We add our experiences to the tales of long ago, and we tell the stories again: God shared dinner with Abraham at Mamre; God ate and drank with Moses and the elders; we knew him at the breaking of bread; Elijah's cup is drained, at this meal, by God.

"Are you able to drink the cup that I drink?" asks Jesus of his faithful ones. For there is also the cup of wrath:

For in the LORD's hand there is a cup,
full of spiced and foaming wine—the LORD pours it
  out—
  and all the wicked of the earth shall drink and
  drain the dregs.
                                                    (Psalm 75)

Enraged Jeremiah demands that the world's evil ones be given the poisonous cup. Yet a stained-glass window in a Paris church depicts the winepress of God; intended to squeeze out the wine from the earth's sour grapes, it is instead pressing down on Christ, and his blood seeps out from his veins into the waiting chalices. And in the waiting room of an oncology surgeon in St. Paul, Minnesota, is a depiction of the Last Supper, the cup being filled with the tears of God and the bloody sweat of Jesus. For the drink poured for Jesus is not only the goblet of Elijah but also the vinegar of God's wrath and sorrow. "Abba, remove this cup from me," he begged.

Among the most revered of Christian artifacts have been the chalices, those great jeweled golden goblets, the ornate designs and engraved scenes fervently trying to make the outside of the cup worthy of its contents. But the wonder is not the spun silver depiction of Caleb and Joshua lugging back to camp a mammoth bunch of grapes, nor the gems which rivaled the sovereign's crown. The wonder is the wine of drinking the new covenant with God, the holy grail of the life of the one who drained the dregs of suffering. "Drink me," the bottle said to Alice: and so we do and, with Alice, are transformed. How impoverished they are who replace such a cup with glass jiggers, as if God were a sip, bottoms-up, a quarter-teaspoon measured out in the prescription of healing me! The four-year-old said, "It's funny: We drink God in the wine." Indeed, the finest, most precious article of our worship ought to be the cup, this container of God, which in pouring Christ into us all pours us into one another and so into God.

O LORD, you are my portion and my cup;
in your presence there is fullness of joy,
and in your right hand are pleasures for evermore.
(Psalm 16)

9

David was first a shepherd, the nomad, the mythic Bedouin who roamed the wilds and lived in a tent and cared for the sheep. The rugged life of compassion, the brute strength of the herdsman, choosing to protect the dirty, stupid sheep: This was David, the shepherd. David was later a king, the authority of the civilized city, the protector of the gates, the judge for the oppressed, a warrior to save the people. He wore a crown and commanded homage. From the chaos of warring towns he moulded a mighty nation: David, the king. David was always a singer, fingering beauty on his harp, shaping praise into a psalm, offering songs for the sheep and for the throne and for the people. David the singer plucked the harp that pacified mad Saul and acclaimed the greatness of God.

So David was the epitome of God's ancient people, the chief of the chosen ones, sign of the promise, most faithful lord. And in a kind of linguistic square dance in which partners get interchanged, it is not only that David is the model Jew because, acclaimed by God, he is shepherd and king and singer, but also that YHWH is God because, acclaimed by David and all the people, God is shepherd and king and singer.

God is shepherd, leading the flock of Israel, tending the ewes, saving the strays, finding pasture, watering the infirm, bringing them home. For David is shepherd in the way that God is shepherd:

> *My shepherd is LORD, I have all I need,*
> *giving me rest in green and pleasant fields,*
> *reviving my soul by finding fresh water,*
> *guiding my ways with a shepherd's care.*
>
> *(Psalm 23)*

God is king, protecting the city, ruling over the people, establishing justice, heeding the poor, sitting on that throne before which we subject ourselves in awe. For David is king only a child king compared to the king that is God:

> *The LORD is King for ever and ever;*
>   *the ungodly shall perish from his land.*
> *The LORD will hear the desire of the humble;*
>   *you will strengthen their heart and your ears shall*
>   *hear;*
> *To give justice to the orphan and oppressed,*
>   *so that mere mortals may strike terror no more.*
>
> *(Psalm 10)*

God is singer, maker of beauty, weaver of harmony, whose melody is grace, whose rhythm is justice. Better yet, God is the song, the only music worth singing, the *cantus firmus* of the universe, the obbligato of salvation.

> *Give thanks, the LORD is good,*
> *Unending is God's love.*
> *Let all who revere the LORD say,*
> *Unending is God's love.*
> *My strength, my song is the LORD,*
> *who has become my Savior.*
>
> *(Psalm 118)*

But we ask: In which direction do the metaphors flow? Is David acclaimed because he is made in the likeness of God, or is God described in recognizable ways because we already honor David? Who is the God beyond the shepherd, the king, the song? Who is the God beyond the metaphors upon which our poems rely?

For there is more to God than David, although D is surely one of the letters for God's name.

Exsultet jam Angelica turba caelorum;
exsultent divina mysteria. . . .

With these words ringing from ancient times down to the present, the deacon proclaims Easter. In most translations in contemporary English, the deacon's poem begins, "Rejoice!", but still the chant is called the Exsultet, the Leaping Up for Joy, a jumping up from the grave in delight.

The poem has its setting: a dark nave, a crowd in the night keeping vigil, a white-robed deacon bearing high a large lit candle. The enormous size of some ancient paschal candle-stands makes us wonder whether the candle would not have been too heavy to be borne. But even nowadays the candle glows high above our heads, a phallic light over the womb waters in the fecund night. Around this single flame gathers the congregation, and the Exsultet is chanted. The angel choirs, the earth and "its ancient darkness," the church, and the congregation are to exult, to leap for joy, at the brilliant splendor, the radiant brightness, of the single candle.

("This one candle?!"

("Well, no, Christ.")

("Well, why not sing to Christ, instead of to the candle?")

("Well, because! Besides, it's not *to* the candle.")

The single candle is an icon before us, becoming other than it is, receiving us other than we are, as the chant transforms words to other than they appear. We proclaim the Exsultet, we leap up for joy because, on this Saturday night, the debt of Adam is repaid; the lamb's blood is smeared on our door; Israel crosses the sea; sinners are restored to holiness; the chains of death are snapped; hell is harrowed; and earth is wed to heaven. The tragedy of Eden is "a happy fault." The morning star, the resurrected Lord, and this single burning candle are superimposed, intermingled; and where our recently purchased paschal candle stops and where Christ takes over, the poem will not say. Thus the deacon, with eyes straining in the darkened church to see the words of the chant, exults over the spectacular brilliance of the room!

> *You, O LORD, are my lamp;*
> *My God, you make my darkness bright.*
>
> *(Psalm 18)*

Easter-day celebrations are blind to this part of God's name, the shining of light in darkness. On the sunny morning, new clothes, Easter bonnets, white lilies, shiny trumpets, daffodil corsages—it is easy to sing about seeds growing into new flowers. But in what is called the dead of night, exulting over one single candle and acclaiming it God's beacon calls for faith in the resurrection.

For in the night it is not so much that we exalt God, giving God glory, singing a song of praise. It is rather that we exult in God as we leap up out of the dark and out from the grave, leap

16

up in God. Not only do we leap up because of God, but we leap up in God: We entombed, but God surrounding our tomb; and so we leap out of death into God. Perhaps, then, God is also the darkness of the night into which we leap, as well as being the candle around which we exult.

> *You will shelter them,*
>> *so that those who love your Name may exult in*
>> *you.*

(Psalm 5)

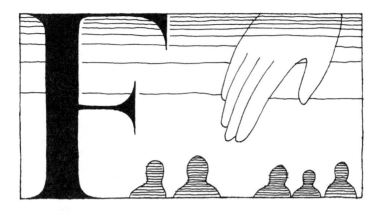

F is a risky letter to use in the name of God. It stands on only one small point and is so top-heavy that all too easily it pitches over and lands crestfallen on its open face. Only by careful attention to posture can an F stand balanced.

F is for father.

Freud suggested that all human beings construct their self-image in conflict with their fathers and that, for male and female alike, mental health or disease can be traced back to child-father relationships. Freud further suggested, then, that the Western god is only a human father projected into the skies by our guilty cultural consciousness and that as we become freed from our captivity to our fathers, we might finally be rid of such a god. To the extent that we do worship great blimps of our father, we are grateful to Freud for puncturing that balloon. But faith pleads an objective God, a God prior to human obsessions, a God beyond our needs, a God whose powerful self-revelation actually corresponds with religious truth. To pull the cotton beard off an uncle playing Santa Claus does not mean that there was never a St. Nicholas who blessed God by giving gold to children.

But there are fathers and fathers.

As a father cares for his children,
so does the LORD care for the godfearing.
(Psalm 103)

Here, father is a stumbling word saying that God saves, that God cares. The boy who comes up smiling to say, "That stupid bunny-rabbit! It stood on the path and growled at me!"—what does the boy mean to say? For often our words, though factually imprecise, are affectively potent. We try to say God is our life, and, among other words, the word "father" comes out.

There is a second father:

[David] will say to me, "You are my Father,
my God, and the rock of my salvation."
(Psalm 89)

We quote the imagery of divine lineage, the ancient metaphor that the sovereign is descendent from God, born of God, ruling for God. So David was child, and Jesus was child, and we, says Paul, are children and heirs. Among the crown jewels Christians have inherited is this ring of images, God as Father King, and we, children of the sovereign, destined to reign. So as we quote the Old Testament, as we try to say we reign through God, the word "father" comes out.

Yet a third. Jesus blasphemes, they argued: How can this man be equal to God? Abba, he calls Almighty God in prayer! Abba, a child's word: daddy, papa. That's my dad, says this carpenter, of the Holy One of Israel. And so, as we try to quote Jesus, as in baptism we take on the mantle of Christ, even this truth is too hard for us. We do not call God papa, but the word "father" comes out.

20

Yet a fourth. There is the mystery that our God is a God for whom relationship is so essential that even within Godself is the vibrancy of intermingling love, a trinity of single-being. And so, as we recall the creeds of the church, as we baptize into the ancient faith, we call the Trinity by its own mysterious names, and the word "father" comes out.

But this F is difficult to balance. It is easy to draw a father as we think a father might be. We catechize, rather unbiblically, that we are to pray to God as Father because we, poor disobedient children, are duty bound to obey our Master. There are prayers evoking the Father which ask God to bless the family and to reproduce some understanding of divine order by making the husband supreme. Women are classed as lesser beings because male sexuality is transferred to the being of God. Stereotypically masculine behavior is holier, preferred, because God is a father. Ah, the unbalanced F.

I taught my three-year-old to pray, "Thank you, God, for being my father; thank you, God, for being my mother. Thank you, God, for being my friend; thank you, God, for being my castle." For some months she requested the prayer daily, and she always concluded, "God is not a castle. God is God." Yes. Nor is God a father. God is God, beyond any and all divine names, and God cracks all names, although we hope, as with crystalline gems, to revere their perfection on our shelf. But safely shelved, divine names become only paste mock-ups if not imbued again and again with the unbounded brilliance of God. So lest we think Jesus' "Father" an easy name, we remember Jesus praying to his Abba from the cross:

My God, my God, why have you forsaken me?
and are so far from my cry
and from the words of my distress?

Yet you are the Holy One,
   enthroned upon the praises of Israel.

(Psalm 22)

So what kind of a father is that?

God's gaze is good, we like to say. For our language assumes that God has eyes, that God sees everything, that God gazes on the faithful. We would hardly draw God as a great nose or a mammoth mouth, but even our God is pictured sometimes as a single open eye in the center of a triangle. That eye of course would never blink, and even when tears would wash it of the world's dust, it would gaze through the tears with penetrating mercy. The native Huichols of central Mexico have taught our children to make "gods' eyes" at summer camp, and whether of Popsicle sticks and yellow yarn or of great woods and fine threads, the sign is the same: the four corners of the earth crossing to mark the place of the gaze of God. And so we like to pray:

The LORD looks down from heaven,
and beholds all the people in the world.
Seated enthroned, the LORD gazes out
on all who dwell on the earth.
Behold, the eye of the LORD is upon the godfearing,
on those who wait for mercy.

(Psalm 33)

I will gaze on you, says God, says the lover to the beloved. My look will not waver; on you I am fixed. And so we get the made-up word "gazebo," as if we were speaking Latin to say "I will gaze," and we build a white canopy in the garden where lovers can gaze at each other and together gaze at the sea. Meanwhile in the nearby cloister the contemplative nun, in love with Jesus, gazes in adoration at the altar, catching her glimpse of God.

But (yes, there is always a but) the gaze of God is not only the beloved one making eyes at her sweetheart. The testimony of the Hebrew people is that a human being cannot endure the prolonged gaze of God. Moses can look only on God's backside, for even the highest human holiness cannot meet the divine eyes. We hide with Adam in the bushes of Eden. We run with Peter from the courtyard. So lest we seek fearlessly to bear the sight of God, we sing a different psalm:

Take your affliction from me;
I am worn down by the blows of your hand.
With rebukes for sin you punish us;
like a moth you eat away all that is dear to us;
truly, everyone is but a puff of wind.
Hear my prayer, O LORD, and give ear to my cry;
hold not your peace at my tears.
Turn your gaze from me, that I may be glad again,
before I go my way and am no more.

(Psalm 39)

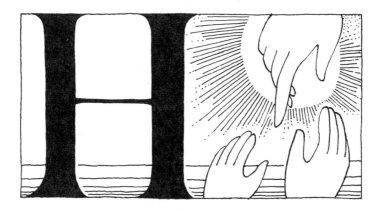

It was March 1, a routine day at the gynecologist's office. By the door there sat a forty-some-year-old Irish Catholic woman, worn, white with the white of illness added to the white of Irish, nine months pregnant with her fifth child: "I've three boys and a girl; we'll call the baby Brian." Even while sitting still, she panted for breath and waved a copy of *People* magazine to cool herself. She had always been constipated during her pregnancies, but this was terrible, this was five days. . . . In a corner sat an old woman, short gray hair, aspirating unevenly; she had been led into the waiting room by a black attendant. So old! How could something still be wrong with her womb? How long has it been since she was a well woman? In another corner was a middle-aged woman, dressed in a gray flannel suit, getting a checkup after a miscarriage. She said she felt rather well, no longer convinced that the physicians and the anesthetist had spent that half hour kicking her in the belly. And in the fourth corner was the inevitable high-school girl, designer jeans, blank face, dazed eyes, walled into loneliness, holding her Dixie cup of urine, awaiting word on a test that would prove positive. The receptionist spoke loudly into the phone: a woman with severe pains, another woman bleeding. Finally into this room of unhealth bounced a new mother for her two-week checkup, grinning her face apart, her newborn squalling until she bared the infant her breast. The nurses exulted: "The baby is lovely! They're always so beautiful after a Cesarean!"

Have pity on me, LORD, for I am weak;
  heal me, LORD, for my bones are racked.

                                                          (Psalm 6)

All this unhealth, and it was March 1, the day George Herbert had died 350 years before:

My flesh began unto my soul in pain,
  Sicknesses cleave my bones;
Consuming agues dwell in ev'ry vein;
  And tune my breath to grones.
Sorrow was all my soul; I scarce beleeved,
Till grief did tell me roundly, that I lived.

All those women and George Herbert pleading for health, for bodies that work: closer than Calcutta is sorrow to the marrow. We plead for the day when the scar is healed and we feel its fierce line no more. We plead for a healthy child, a healthy mother.

And so we plead for God, God our health, God who sometimes gives health, but not always—no, not even to those who pray most piously—some health to some people, as if health were each single time a miracle, a gift of God's self made on this special occasion to a people more acquainted with pain.

Or more: to plead for God as if we really trusted that God is Health, that being in God is being in health, little and big death notwithstanding.

Let your ways be known upon earth,
your saving health among all nations.
Let the peoples praise you, O God;
let all the peoples praise you.

(Psalm 67)

Because of the incarnation there are icons, say Orthodox Christians.

Of course we cannot draw a picture of God! Nonsense, to think we can depict divinity! Yet God became human, and so it is almost as if God wants to be seen, God choosing a form which can be drawn, God approving the need of our curious eyes. God is made known in the incarnation, God enfleshed as a human person: "and the Word was God." Christ is the image of God, Christ the icon of divinity. In the same way that Christ is the human through whom one sees divinity, the icon is the exercise of religious faith. The iconographer paints Christ, Mary, and the saints, their humanity elongated beyond nature, their sanctified eyes drawing us into the depths of that redeemed soul, the depiction a way of adoring the incarnate God, the infinity beyond. The image glimpses humankind on its way to becoming divine by imaging Christ, who was divinity in the flesh. So, say these Christians, we see God behind and through the icon. The God of the incarnation is imaged in the icon.

There is an icon in Madison, Wisconsin, painted more than 400 years ago and 10,000 miles away. Now it is there, a great triptych, the center of which are Mary and John the Baptist beseeching with their prayers the enthroned Christ, dressed as an archpriest. Now, really! Jesus of Nazareth a priest, with chasuble, stole, and jeweled crown? The sides of the triptych tell why: Icons of the twelve great feasts of the church attend the reigning Christ. ("Wisdom: attend!") For in these events here recalled—the annunciation, the nativity, the presentation, and on through to the raising of Adam and Eve from hell—there is an image of God worshiped, the liturgy a kind of icon itself, the festivals of Christ providing an image of God, a way to see the God beyond historical event or liturgical celebration.

"To represent the God of Sabaoth (that is, the Father) on icons with a gray beard, with his only Son on his lap, and a dove between them, is exceedingly absurd and unseemly," spoke the Great Moscow Council in 1667. How icons pictured God was to recall the Genesis story of God's first appearance to the faithful, when God came for dinner to the tent of Abraham and Sarah. God comes, God speaks, but isn't it three persons we see? But the narrative calls them angels! How is it that we cannot know with whom we speak? Who is this who so mysteriously escapes our categories? So the icon of the Holy Trinity pictures the three angels who ate with Abraham and Sarah, three beings of the created order through whom God chose to be seen.

This God we worship—looking for Adam, dining with Sarah and Abraham, showing Moses the divine backside, born in Jesus, alive in the saints, proclaiming in the icon—this God must want to be seen. God in the word? No less, say some, God in the icon. The Hebrews were right: We do not sculpt God. But there is Christ, the icon of God, with whom we have shared a meal. And there is my icon of the presentation, a tiny theophany, through which we glimpse God.

Deliver me, O LORD, by your hand
*   from those whose portion in life is this world.*
At my vindication I shall see your face;
*   when I awake, I shall be satisfied, beholding your*
*   likeness.*

(Psalm 17)

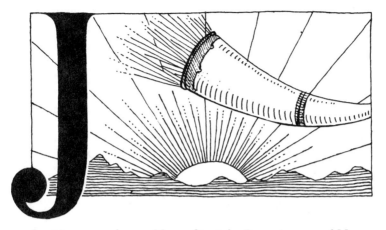

Leviticus says that on Mount Sinai the LORD instructed Moses in the way of the Jubilee. Every seven years the land would have a sabbatical: no crops planted, not even straggling shoots harvested. It was a year to rest in the LORD. But once every fifty years would come the Jubilee of Jubilees, and in that year the land lying fallow would be the least of the signs of the time of the LORD. The trumpet would blow, and families would reassemble. Land sold to pay off loans would be given back. Houses that the rich had acquired from the poor would be returned. People indentured to settle great debts would be released. It was a free redemption, all the way around, debts paid off because completely forgiven.

So here we have a man; perhaps he is named Joshua. Middle-aged, bonded as a child to pay off his family debt, he works the quarries to hack out stone, or perhaps his service requires that he watch the gates through the night. His only thought: the Jubilee of Jubilees. Will that year really come? Will all the people recognize it, acclaim it, live out its spirit? No, such a time for freedom must be only an ancient memory or worse yet, a myth from olden times about the possibility of peace. Yet Joshua hopes. He waits each night for the morning star. He hopes for forgiveness of all debts; he hopes to arise from the pit; he hopes for a new morning to shine; he hopes for the mercy of freedom. He knows, in his prayers, that in hoping for the Jubilee of Jubilees he is hoping for God. For the coming of such joy is only the arrival of God.

> *Out of the depths have I called to you, O LORD;*
> *LORD, hear my voice;*
> > *let your ears consider well the voice of my*
> > > *supplication.*
> *I wait for the LORD; my soul is waiting;*
> > *in the LORD'S word is my hope.*
> *My soul waits for the LORD,*
> *more than watchmen for the morning,*
> > *more than watchmen for the morning.*
> *O Israel, wait for the LORD,*
> > *for with the LORD there is mercy.*
> *There is plenteous redemption with the LORD,*
> > *who shall redeem Israel from all their sins.*
> > > > > > > *(Psalm 130)*

K . . . K. What does K say about God? Key, king, koinonia . . . until there in the unabridged dictionary was "K, Kuphar, a small round boat of willow covered with skins used on the Euphrates." Well.

> *By the waters of Babylon we sat down and wept,*
> *when we remembered you, O Zion.*
>
> *(Psalm 137)*

Twenty-five hundred years ago they were there, Jews exiled in Babylon, weeping into the river Euphrates. They could not drown their songs in the Euphrates—the river is too shallow— but their joys were flooded away. Singing the LORD'S song in a strange land, how they would have wished for such a small round boat—a kuphar—to carry them safely up the river and back to the Holy Land. God had provided the willows lining the Euphrates. Perhaps God would provide also the skins: Hadn't Adam and Eve received their needed skins from the LORD? One can hear the faithful, choking on Zion's songs, groaning, ah! for a kuphar, a kuphar to take us home.

35

It is still the same. Along with our praises rises the plea that a boat will come our way, taking us from slavery back to our own free land. We beg for a ship to save us from the stormy wind by sailing us back to safety.

Then were they glad because of the calm;
  the LORD brought them to the harbor they were
    bound for.

(Psalm 107)

One boat has been granted, one kuphar for our Euphrates, one ark for our flood. We sit each week on its wooden benches, in that nave of ours, and sail home to God, in God. For the kuphar God sends is the kuphar God is.

It will take us a while to get to L.

L begins back in the burning bush, when from the flame God's name ignites: YHWH. The consonants spell out the sacred tetragrammaton, the name by which God is known by the chosen ones, and pious Jews revere the holy initials as part of the mystery of God's self. Contemporary scholars quarrel over the translation of the ambiguous letters: I am? I will be? There on Horeb, the mountain of God, a shepherd hears the divine name spelled with a Y: but we are not certain what the name means.

The rabbis who wrote the tetragrammaton never did, however, pronounce it. They read, instead, Adonai. For the given name, God's first name, they substituted a title of respect: the One who rules, the sovereign One. God's personal name is replaced by a mark of our subservience: We are the people, God is Adonai. The Hebrew title is part of Israel's social order. Now in God's naming are heard cultural overtones, God in the image of the masculine master of the people. The Y becomes an A: but we are not certain when the alteration occurred or why that title was chosen.

In the first century before Christ, the Jews who spoke Greek translated the Hebrew scriptures into their vernacular; but how to render Adonai? The choice was Kyrios, the supreme authority, the divine ruler, the lord. For so did their culture in its panegyrics name the king: the emperor is kyrios. From Y to A to K: The title of a male monarch is now collided with the name of God.

There is more about K. The writers of the New Testament, living still in a land where the emperor was kyrios, called Jesus Kyrios. "My Kyrios and my God," Thomas calls the resurrected Christ. So if we thought we have unraveled the chain of letters, there is now a new knot: The name of the burning bush is bound into the title awarded Jesus of Nazareth.

In 404 Jerome completed his translation of the Bible from Hebrew and Greek into Latin. In his day the word Dominus was the title of the emperor, and, by extension, of lesser lords in the emerging feudal system, and Jerome takes that word, Dominus, to translate Kyrios. To our ears the word has a heaviness about it: domination, we think. YHWH is Dominus, Jesus is Dominus. From Y to A to K to D, the ambiguous verb in the burning bush is now the name of the Roman emperor. The Latin liturgical prayers which begin "Dominus Deus" are addressing, after all, YHWH Elohim, God of the Torah.

The Anglo-Saxon word was originally hlafweard, then hlaford: the loaf-ward, the bread-keeper, the provider. From Latin into English, Dominus becomes Lord. At least in the Anglo-Saxon the sense of obligation lies in the hlaford: He must offer the bread. In modern English the sense of obligation is transferred to those who serve their Lord.

So we are at L, spelled LORD when it substitutes for YHWH, and spelled Lord when it acclaims Jesus as Messiah.

The Christian creed relies on this language: the LORD is God, Jesus is Lord. Prayers are addressed to the LORD "through your Son, Jesus Christ our Lord." And when in the liturgy we say "The Lord be with you," we are not certain of whom we are speaking.

Throughout this convoluted history are two constants: that human language can only feebly choose some title of distinction from one's meager culture with which to name God; and that at the core of God's name is ultimate, profound mystery. The being of God is a center which human language cannot probe; we can only orbit around at some distance. So we would do well somehow to recapture the mystery of the tetragrammaton. For Jesus' being Lord is the scandal of Christianity only if the word LORD means, above all, the sacred being of God, not some medieval landowner all dressed up on madrigal night.

> *The LORD said to my Lord, "Sit at my right hand,*
> *until I make your enemies your footstool."*
> *The LORD has sworn and will not recant:*
> *"You are a priest for ever after the order of*
> *Melchizedek."*
> *The Lord who is at your right hand*
> *will smite kings in the day of his wrath;*
> *he will rule over the nations.*
>
> *(Psalm 110)*

Once upon a time there was a young girl living in a land of terror. The king had wickedly decreed to murder the boy babies of the aliens. Now the young girl had a baby brother, newly born, still weeping quietly, held constantly at his mother's breast so that his crying was quickly stilled. But the day his cry became too loud, his mother decided to hide the child. She made a basket of rushes, painted it watertight, and floated it in the river, hiding it in the rushes alongside the shore. The young girl had the task of watching. She was to babysit, to guard the helpless boy, to embrace the child with her eyes, at least. And the girl did well: Her brother Moses was saved. She protected him from evil, she devised a rescue, she brought him home again to warmth and milk and life. The young girl's name was Miriam.

Much later there was a woman of God to whom were given three children. Without much assistance from her husband, she strove to raise her children in a life of grace. But she was plagued especially by her eldest and wayward son. She prayed for that son, disciplined him, and followed him when he ran away. She offered him love, always more love, wept over his foolishness, and invited him to God. And the woman did well: Her son Augustine was saved. She had taught him to love; she had forgiven him. She persevered beyond all expectation and brought him home to the church and to baptism and to life. The woman's name was Monica.

You are the LORD;
do not withhold your compassion from me;
*   let your love and your faithfulness keep me safe for*
*   ever.*
For innumerable troubles have crowded upon me;
my sins have overtaken me, and I cannot see;
*   they are more in number than the hairs of my*
*   head,*
*   and my heart fails me.*
Be pleased, O LORD, to deliver me;
O LORD, make haste to help me.
You are my helper and my deliverer;
*   do not tarry, O my God.*

(Psalm 40)

Miriam; Monica. A girl who saved her brother; a woman who loved her son. Moses is freed from innumerable troubles; the sins did not overtake Augustine. Miriam, Monica: In case you have not guessed, two of the names for God.

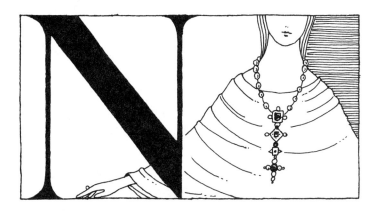

N is for necklace, the necklace from the Woman of Samaria.

A necklace from the Woman of Samaria?

There was in the 1850s, in New Lebanon, New York, a Shaker woman who, like several other Shaker women, recorded her religious ecstasies and gave notation to her spiritual inventions in a unique form—half drawing, half handwriting, fragmented, primitive, precise, charming. Her drawing is a kind of reverse illuminated manuscript, with the text illuminating the pictures. One of her works, entitled "A Type of Mother Hannah's Pocket Handkerchief," depicts a vision from the divine, from Holy Mother Wisdom herself. The drawing has the familiar Shaker symbols: geometric designs, heart-shaped leaves, fanciful flowers, bizarre birds, all labeled with the strangest of phrases. Here is "A Cage of Singing birds, from Sarah of Old," and the "fan of Mother Hannah, to blow away buffetings." For Holy Mother Wisdom says in this epiphany, "In my Wisdom I will cause to be taken from you the choicest of treasures, for a season. And again they shall return to you greatly beautified and increased seven fold." One such treasure pictured here is "A Necklace from the Woman of Samaria."

N, necklace. Within that community which forbade both necklaces and husbands stands this sign of a divine treasure to come, worn not now, oh no, but returned later by divine Wisdom: a necklace for this Samaritan floozy turned exemplar. When she of the five husbands enters God's eternity, there awaits even for her a necklace from God, one jewel for each marriage promise, one gold link for each other failure forgiven.

And so in the end we too will put on the necklace of God. We will wear divinity, we will don God. Christ wore out his rags so that we will wear God's radiance. We are to be adorned by God, arrayed in God, encircled by a lace of grace. Now we stand naked in good company: Eve and Adam, awaiting leather tunics; the people of Israel, their outfits forty years old; the wedding guest, requiring a robe; the newly baptized, dripping with God. As a bride adorns herself with her jewels, the Woman of Samaria fastens her necklace.

First the shroud, then the crown; first the winding-sheet, then the white raiment. Like the soldier at the cross, we win the cloak of God. How did Paul say it? What is mortal must be clothed with immortality. And what will that be like—a chasuble of cloth-of-gold? A dazzling white robe? A homespun tunic, woven without seam? A coat of mail, gems silvered together?

No. It will not be some outfit that the Woman of Samaria will wear. Indeed, her necklace will be the very self of God.

Hear, O LORD, and have mercy upon me;
  O LORD, be my helper.
You have turned my wailing into dancing;

you have put off my sack-cloth and clothed me with
   joy.
Therefore my heart sings to you without ceasing;
   O LORD my God, I will give you thanks for ever.
                                                (Psalm 30)

The oboe's sound resists description. The words we use—nasal, twangy—connote unpleasantness. But the expert oboist (and if you have heard only the oboe in the high school band, you have not heard what I have heard), the consummate oboist, one of the world's best, creating that extraordinary tone, perhaps laying a high G# pianissimo on the very edge of your hearing—that sound is not *nasal*. That oboe—odd, penetrating—leaves the air altered. Stunned, one keeps vigil for the advancing sound by not breathing. Standards for sound have now changed. All hearing is now in relationship to that oboe solo.

But let's stop talking about it. Talk about music, like talk about God, is too easily vague babble. Words should say only, "Listen to that oboe."

One September evening I heard the principal oboist of the New York Philharmonic perform a solo passage in a contemporary composition. And I said, "There is more about God in that oboe than in most sermons I've ever heard." But lest you think me only another of those church musicians who prattle on as if the liturgy is best thought of as a sacred concert and singing a cantata better than proclaiming the lessons, let me explain.

It was not that there was gospel in that oboe. Christ was not proclaimed, and incarnation is not about musical instruments. But the oboe sounded out against shallow biblical interpretations, sermons in which the vision of God is limited and our vision, then, further obscured. At least with the oboe the universe had to expand in order to contain the sound. Perception itself had trembled. Words had stopped. The oboe had suggested the absolute. And so, unlike trivial sermons, the oboe had pointed toward God.

Being pointed toward God is not everything; it alone cannot save. But it is at least something. It is something worth the tremble.

> *The voice of the LORD is a powerful voice;*
> * the voice of the LORD is a voice of splendor.*
> *The voice of the LORD breaks the cedar trees;*
> * the LORD breaks the cedars of Lebanon.*
> *The voice of the LORD makes the oak trees writhe*
> * and strips the forests bare.*
> *And in the temple of the LORD*
> * all are crying, "Glory!"*
>
> *(Psalm 29)*

"The pinions of God will protect you."

P is for peacock, the paradise bird of stunning beauty, whose tail has a hundred eyes and whose flesh, it is said, does not decay. And so God is a peacock, immortality and glory and iridescent dress.

P is for pelican. The story says that in rage the father pelican murdered his young and that the mother pelican revived her children by sprinkling on them the blood she let from her own breast. In his hymn "Adoro Te," Thomas Aquinas recalls the myth by calling Jesus "pie pellicane." (But Cardinal Newman edited that out, leaving Jesus only as the pure font.) And so God is a pelican, feeding her children with her own blood.

P is for phoenix. After living 500 years on the tears of incense, the phoenix builds a death nest and sets itself on fire, from the ashes of which, three days later, emerges the new young phoenix; for there is only one phoenix alive at any one time. Its plumage is brilliant scarlet and gold. And so God is a phoenix, the only one, which offers itself for self-immolation and three days later is revived for life.

49

God's pinions: a nimbus shimmering blue-green; a bloody white breast; scarlet, then ash, then gold. A God with feathers? Divine plumes? Yet we sing, "Lord Jesus, since you love me, now spread your wings above me," and God describes the escape from Egypt as a flight on eagle's wings. That eagle flies through the psalms, the mother eagle pushing her young out of the nest to teach them to fly, but swooping down underneath to catch them with her wings in case they fall. Perhaps in the end-time authors and poets, still compulsively writing about the divine names, will be graced with a quill pen plucked from the plumage of God.

> *Be merciful to me, O God, be merciful,*
> *for I have taken refuge in you;*
>> *in the shadow of your wings will I take refuge*
>> *until this time of trouble has gone by.*
>>> *(Psalm 57)*

What if our God were Queen of heaven?

If our God were Queen of heaven, we could burn incense to her and bake cakes for her, and our adoration would be acceptable.

If our God were Queen of heaven, her crown would rest on hair long and curly and rainbowed, and we could grab on to that hair as we nursed and so be saved from falling. Her shining face, smooth and clear as light, would enliven the universe. And when we were poor, the Queen would take from her necklace flowing with pearls and opals and every colored gem perhaps an amber to fill our needs. The resplendent gold of her majestic robe would be what we call the sun, and the sheen of her nightdress the moon. Her rule would reach to the deepest corners of the darkness; her beauty would rout the devils and her wisdom rear the world. Her royal blood would give us divinity. Our being born again in God would be a nativity from the divine womb, God's labor an agony of necessity; for we know it is the essence of the reign of our Queen to love with mercy. Our death would be, as with all babies, a going home to mother. Our life would be, as with heirs apparent, following in the train of the Queen.

Hebrew poetry and Christian metaphor have made our divine Sovereign only a king. But a king, say the fairy tales, requires a queen. The universe must be balanced. So the court was filled: The Queen is Mary, bearing the king's son and wedded to Christ the King. She was the first to enter God's reign, from the moment of her birth and since the moment of her death accepting God's crown of grace. Like Queen Esther, she takes our petitions to the throne. And again, the Queen is the church, which is sometimes a virgin, sometimes a whore, always the desired, the divine lover, married to God and reigning with God over all of creation. The rabbis too played word games, and God reigned as king with the divine spirit, Ruah, or with law, Torah, or with wisdom, Hokmah, or with the holy space of divine presence, Shekinah—these feminine nouns a kind of queen attending the royal throne.

But it could have been another set of images as well. The Sovereign of heaven and earth is also a womb of mercy, a majesty of grace and beauty, one who creates the royal children out of herself:

> *In the beauty of holiness have I begotten you,*
> *like dew from the womb of the morning.*
>
> *(Psalm 110)*

The people of God could be a symbolic man, perhaps the Human One of Daniel's vision, who serves the divine monarch by accompanying her pangs of life-giving. Or the Sovereign could be the Queen and we all be Mary, divine generation, dynasty of Amazons, sharing in the world's labor: the first birth, like creation, a birth unto death; and the rebirth, like the resurrection, a birth unto life.

The beauty of the Sovereign has terrified the world. She has borne us in pain and nursed us with care; and we, like Jewish children, carry her blood and are royal from rebirth in her. For our God is Queen of all the earth, and adoration of her splendor is our life.

To you I lift up my eyes,
  to you enthroned in the heavens.
As the eyes of servants look to the hand of their
    masters,
  and the eyes of a maid to the hand of her mistress,
So our eyes look to the LORD our God,
  until the LORD show us mercy.

                                        (Psalm 123)

But it is all so many words, noises grunting out adoration, a cat purring affection, babble ill-informed and misdirected, an alphabet shouted out into the abyss, preceded by a prayer that the angels will shape it into a canticle of praise.

When suppertime came and all my fair-skinned family had soaked up enough sun to make us miserable, we would leave the sandy beach and hike up to the great rocky point where picnics would be spread out on boulders. I was young, and I would choose my own private crag, one partway into the salty water, so my toes could play with the barnacles, and there I would sup atop a rock in the sea.

It is harder, now, to find rocks so satisfying as were those boulders, water splashing up against my personal palisade between the poison ivy and the sea. And not me alone: The stories are filled with an archetypal search for the rock, the rock that is higher than I, the rock on which to build, the rock that makes me secure. Even in the desert the desire for a rock is there: stone against the shifting sands, a shade from the scalding sun. And to the Hebrews' surprise, the rock splits open, and from the great fissure gushes water, both rock and water at once, so that the people might survive. And the rabbis later said that the rock followed the people around the desert for all forty years.

The disciples too needed a rock, and as Paul elucidates the ancient wilderness travels, "the rock was Christ." And so Christ found, or founded, a rock, and on Peter was built a city, and Rome became a kind of rock as Jerusalem had been, the foundation stone of a nation and the navel of the world. Also, from this rock flowed water, the water in all those ancient baptistries now dry to tourists' cameras, as the water had flowed from his side the hour the Rock was cleft.

Not only the water, but we too are born of the cleft rock: Moses' psalm in Deuteronomy reminds us of the Rock who bears and begets us. We are born of the Rock that is God; we stand on the Rock that is Christ; we live by the water outpouring; and at our death the rock of our tomb will be the doorway to God.

Tremble, earth, at the presence of the LORD,
  at the presence of the God of Jacob,
Who turned the hard rock into a pool of water
  and flint-stone into a flowing spring.

  (Psalm 114)

For as Psalm 62 repeats,

God alone is my rock and my salvation,
  my stronghold, so that I shall not be shaken.

The images of warfare have lost their allure. The cry of the patriot, "Better dead than red," sounds like ancient rhetoric, misguided values from an earlier time when nations were insular and bombs unknown. That was all right for Beowulf, but not for those of us attracted more by the bishops' appeal for nuclear disarmament than by the medals on a soldier's uniform. With no bomb damage in our neighborhood, we pray for victims we see on television, and we argue over how best to respond to devastation an ocean away, or we read novels about the days after the final war. World War II was different: My uncle died in that valor which saved the world from a madman and from the vipers hatching beneath him. Good and evil were more recognizable there than from the trenches of Flanders or ' the jungles of Vietnam. But even there—remember Hiroshima?—there was no glory in war to captivate us.

But our psalms come from another time. War was hardly less hideous then, wounding face to face, with no painkillers available. But the psalms remain, packed full of swords and shields, slings and spears, the shattering of cities and the

57

slaying of soldiers. God is the one who trains for battle; God is the one who fights the harshest; God is the one to whom victory is due. God of Sabaoth, we acclaim: that is, the lord of a host of angelic armies, destroying the enemy so that one people can live. What can our language do with all these metaphors of war? What is here besides our utter distaste? One image survives from all this military science: God as stronghold.

My eyes are fixed on you, O my Strength;
*   for you, O God, are my stronghold.*
My merciful God comes to meet me;
*   God will let me look in triumph on my enemies.*
Slay them, O God, lest my people forget;
*   send them reeling by your might*
*   and put them down, O LORD our shield.*
(Psalm 59)

Stronghold: God as a fastness for us in fear; God as a keep for our treasure; God as a citadel after the climb; God as a tower situated so high that I can see the safest path; God as a fortress whose walls resist attack. So is God a stronghold. God is not only the weapons of war but the protection from war. In this stronghold, using the arms God provides, we live secure. For the arms God offers are God's own arms, which by enfolding us in godly life make our life the more human. For the stronghold of God is the divine embrace. We are held through the night of tears; we are caught up as we call into the depths; we delight to be hugged by the bear who is God. "Hold me up, and I shall be safe," says the psalmist, and so Peter is pulled up from the water by the outstretched arms of Christ.

But finally, there in the psalms, the stronghold becomes a walled garden of peace:

The LORD of hosts is with us;

the God of Jacob is our stronghold.
There is a river whose streams make glad the city of
  God,
  the holy habitation of the Most High.
Come now and look upon the works of the LORD,
  what awesome things God has done on earth.
It is the LORD who makes war to cease in all the
  world,
  who breaks the bow, and shatters the spear,
  and burns the shields with fire.
The LORD of hosts is with us;
  the God of Jacob is our stronghold.

(Psalm 46)

A stronghold is not only a means to war and a protection from war, but also the end of war. God is not only victory, but also peace. The image is more than we first believed.

God's grove of trees.

The tree of life set in Eden, the tree from which we have not yet tasted. But an old legend says that Seth took a seed from that sacred tree and planted it in the grave in Father Adam's mouth. From that seed grew a towering tree around which hovered healing powers; from that tree was built a wooden bridge over the waters at Siloam (and there the Queen of Sheba prophesied a coming glory); from that ramshackle bridge's scrap lumber was finally constructed a cross, which when exhumed by pious Helena restored a dead man to life—the true cross.

Was the tree a gopher tree, lumber for Noah's ark?

Was this tree of life a tamarisk tree, which along with Sarah's tomb, was all Abraham owned in the promised land?

Was this tree of life a palm tree, shading wise Deborah as she judged God's people Israel?

Was the tree a cedar, becoming one of the walls of God's house, the temple in Jerusalem? Or perhaps a cypress, used for the sanctified floor?

Was it perhaps the broom tree under which rested Elijah before he walked up to the mountain of God?

Was the tree an apple tree, hovering over the lovers, she singing a canticle, his upraised trunk spilling over and filling his love with fruit?

And what kind of tree was Jesse's tree, appearing dried up but sheltering a stump, now a twig, now a branch, finally a tree of life?

Was Jesse's tree the fig tree under which Nathaniel sat, only to be found and named by the Messiah?

Was Jesse's tree the sycamore, up which half-pint Zacchaeus would climb to catch a glimpse of God?

Perhaps the tree is the olive tree of God's people, into which we broken branches are grafted?

Most likely the tree is all these: gopher, tamarisk, palm, cedar, cypress, broom, apple and fig, sycamore and olive, and yet two more. For the tree in the city of God at the end of time grows twelve different fruits, and its leaves are for the healing of the nations: a sacred woodland from a single trunk.

Over my desk hangs a reproduction of Hannah Cohoon's "Tree of Life." Hannah Cohoon, who showed up one day with her two children ("no record was found of her marriage," the museum plaque found it necessary to say) in Hancock, Massachusetts, joined the Shaker community there, and is known to us today by name, as precious few Shakers are, because she painted religious symbols. Hannah's drawings are art: this picture a mighty tree with checkered leaves and fruit round and full, greens and orange and gold, like fecund sunflowers, the leaves and fruits far too large for such a slender trunk, but somehow perfectly balanced in a holy air. The Shakers revered the Tree of Life, which they, the elect, would enjoy—not now, but some day.

At the Frick Museum are some unpublished drawings for *Pilgrim's Progress* by William Blake. And while we bemoan all those bearded old men that Blake drew for God, we are struck silent by his depiction of the Tree of Life, sheltering the pilgrim Christian on his journey. For it clearly is a tree— roots, trunk, branches and leaves and fruit; but this tree of life illustrates a passage in which Christian has a vision of the cross. For so it has been in Christian symbolism, that the bountiful tree and the dread tree are one, that the tree of God is both Paradise and Calvary. In Acts, Peter already says that "He was hanged on a *tree*." And so Simone Weil writes of living "naked and nailed to the Tree of Life."

The tree of our God is the cross; our Yggdrasil—that mythic Norse ash tree binding earth and heaven and hell—is the crucifix. Bonaventure's "Tree of Life" makes the branches of the great tree the truths of the mystery of Christ. Yet the cross becomes one not only with the tree of life but also with the tree of knowledge of good and evil, that tree which in confirming the humanity of Eve and Adam gave them death. Did John, at the foot of the cross, catch sight of the serpent, slithering in the shadows of the taboo crosspiece? For on Passion Sunday we affirm that the one "who by a tree overcame might by a tree be overcome."

As the tree is Christ, so we become trees:

The righteous shall flourish like a palm tree,
    and shall spread abroad like a cedar of Lebanon.
Those who are planted in the house of the LORD
    shall flourish in the courts of our God;
They shall still bear fruit in old age;

they shall be green and succulent.

(Psalm 92)

But the tree is Christ; so the tree is God.

It is the LORD who watches over you;
* the LORD is your shade at your right hand.*
The LORD shall preserve you from all evil;
* the LORD shall keep you safe.*

(Psalm 121)

Would that most artists had left the angels off their canvases and out of their marble! Armored goddesses, robed young men, flying beasties, feminine beauties, even toddler angels with pink winglets! These silly representations are glued on our brains, and we cannot hear of angels without remembering wholly inadequate Christmas cards. Such art at the least diminishes our imagination and, at worst, renders the word "angels" powerless in our religious language.

In the ancient stories, one is never sure whether it is God or an angel who is present. The angel, as a representation of the might of God, a bearer of God's grace, is a manner of Godself being among us. Samson's parents exclaim their terror at meeting an angel of the LORD by saying, "We have seen God." Angels are ways of God's being seen, a step toward God's presence. In many biblical tales they figure as the ears and mouth and hands of God.

There are (some say) four archangels: Michael, slayer of the dragon; Gabriel, guardian of Paradise; Raphael, healer and guide; and finally, Uriel. Of Uriel—meaning God's fire—little is known, and the name itself comes only from apocryphal Jewish writings which never made their way onto Christian bookshelves. U is for Uriel, the noncanonical archangel, one of the four who hold up the throne of God. They say it is Uriel who polices Eden's tree of life, who wrestled with Jacob, who killed Egypt's firstborn, who slew Sennacherib's army, who blockades Hades. Some say it was God who warned Noah of the coming flood, but others say God sent Uriel on this deathly task. Uriel is the dark arm of God, the dread news, the discipline and the struggle. Vengeance is mine, says the LORD. Uriel, the hand of God that holds the line on grace, the eyes of God which foresee destruction, and the mouth of God which speaks punishment, has not made a splash in Christianity, in which the divine sea tends to be all life and goodness, sweetness and light.

But the fiery Uriel is burning up God's enemies on every side, melting the wicked as if they were made of wax. And despite the more simpleminded psalms, God's flames burn also the faithful:

How long will you be angry, O LORD?
will your fury blaze like fire for ever?

(Psalm 79)

We appliqué cute flames onto our Pentecost vestments—but the consuming fire which is godly Uriel is hardly some blessed can of Sterno keeping our fondue bubbly. We tend to explain away Luther's enslavement to the terror of God's judgment. But though we might call his fears obsessive, we dare not conclude that there is no judgment of God. It is dangerous to say, "See here, see there," and equate the disasters around us with God's avenging fire, but we must not imagine that God's flames have gone out. Indeed, the burning martyrs said that on Good Friday as well as on Pentecost the fire of God was blazing. Uriel was the angel who came to minister on Calvary.

The Psalms give us words to pray for Uriel's fire:

Fight those who fight me, O LORD;
attack those who are attacking me.
Let them be like chaff before the wind,
and let the angel of the LORD drive them away.
Let their way be dark and slippery,
and let the angel of the LORD pursue them.
(Psalm 35)

Before we can pray for fire on others we must be ready to expect some burns ourselves. To believe that Uriel can act, we must admit that one of God's arms can strike. Indeed, even if we are horrified by such prayers for vengeance, we ought to remember Sodom and Gomorrah, when the smoke of the land went up like smoke from a furnace. For the stories do say that Uriel is there, a fire of consuming rage, one of the four messengers of God.

Once there was a magnificent mountain, the kind that postcards depict, a sight fit for mooning poets or the lone adventurer: the meadow grasses and wild flowers, the pines and streams, the mirror lake, and—displacing the clouds, perhaps holding up the sky itself—the green and purple and finally white shape of the classic mountain summit. Photographers would await a clear day, and thanks to the camera even faraway folks rejoiced before such a picture, delighting to know that in this world of chaos and ugliness there was such a place as this living rainbow of natural balance. Here is what the word "halcyon" is about. Here is natural perfection.

The name of this mountain is Mount St. Helens, and photographers passing by on May 18, 1980, caught the other half of all this stunning beauty. All was over; for decades the place will be desolate. Now the mountain peak itself is blown off, and every tree and flower incinerated by the devastating volcanic heat. The lake has actually disappeared. All color was enwrapped in a gray shroud, and even 3000 miles away the New York sky was soured by that mountain's belch. We who are so smart about the ways of nature, who claim to understand the volcanic process, stood quietly, filtering our breath, stunned by this image of destruction. And although we have logged its dozen subsequent eruptions, measured the grit, calculated the flaming rocks, and analyzed the steam, we for at least some moments experienced a primal terror, for this volcano is greater than we.

Insurance companies seldom grant protection against volcanic damage. The total destruction is uninsurable, and curiously the event is termed "an act of God," a disaster beyond human forethought, a catastrophe outpacing precaution. All calculation and statistics are dumbed by the volcano, devastation beyond reckoning.

Beyond. Beyond. If the spectacle of the mountain's glory is beyond our description, yet more so is the horror of the ash.

Beyond. Beyond.

Some have suggested that many of scripture's images are passé and its language obsolete because it was common, in those olden days, to describe God as the One beyond: beyond what we understand, beyond what we have, beyond what we are. El Shaddai was Abraham's name for God: the God of the mountain peak, God as unfathomable as that distant glory, as mighty as a mount with its power and its beauty. The tradition has translated El Shaddai as only "Almighty God"; the image has been lost. The mountain—which now we scale with climbing equipment and measure with laboratory instruments—is dismissed, and the unambiguous adjective "almighty" substituted and so commonly and thoughtlessly spoken that a child might think that "almighty" is God's first name. Almighty: a vague modifier, especially inadequate to answer the question it itself suggests: Why does God, that God of all might, permit evil in the world? God of the mountain, rather, offers a specific image, a picture of mystery, dearness but otherness, the beloved yet unknown summit of the land.

The image of God of the mountain is not, fortunately, only an idyll, a crag for Wordsworth to contemplate while strolling in the meadow. The God beyond is also the mountain beyond, the end of the mountain, the volcano itself.

The earth reeled and rocked;
*   the roots of the mountains shook;*
*   they reeled because of God's anger.*
Smoke arose from God's nostrils
and a consuming fire from the mouth of the LORD,
*   with hot burning coals blazing forth.*
The LORD was enwrapped in darkness,
*   cloaked in dark waters and thick clouds.*
From the brightness of God's presence, through the
*   clouds,*
*   burst hailstones and coals of fire.*
The LORD thundered out of heaven;
*   the voice of the Most High spoke out.*

(Psalm 18)

God is not the good and pleasant mountain: God is God, the volcano. God-as-mountain talk is mush unless it is mixed with God-as-volcano, just as theology of reconciliation is foolishness unless first there is terror before the God beyond.

God is still beyond: the volcano laying waste our daisies, destroying our idylls. No small task, this: to find images in the modern consciousness for power beyond. Perhaps we could talk of space: not our local space littered with used-up space-ships, but the space beyond the space beyond, the going-out-forever past the solar systems, the never-endingness, the no-edge to the universe, the space from which we have not yet seen light. Not God as the cloud's silver lining, but God as a black hole, the star mass with gravity so great that not only can its light not escape, but its darkness in the end will engulf the universe. Not God as the rays of the sun, but God as the center of the sun.

The scribes wrote, "In the beginning God created. . . ." At first it was enough to give God's title, just "God," the God who is God, and to declare that God created the world. But language moves toward specificity: What we believe to be significant we distinguish linguistically from neighbors near and far. So the simple noun God was soon found to be meager, insufficient.

So to the question seeking discrimination, "But how did God create the world?" the ancient Hebrews sang a clarification:

God who by wisdom made the heavens,
whose mercy endures for ever.

(Psalm 136)

What is it about God that created the world? Wisdom. What did God use to create the world? Divine wisdom alone. Now we have a handle on this untouchable God: Wisdom. Why, we know about wisdom!—the workings of mind meshed with compassion. We can understand a little bit, at least, of God: Wisdom.

So much did divine wisdom occupy Hebrew imaginations that a figure is born, a mighty woman springing fully armed from the Hebrew poet's head: Lady Wisdom herself, whom God created first in the primeval time of creating. Lady Wisdom was God's companion, God's help, meet for creating the universe. The Hebrew writers prize her judgment, her stature, her beauty. This first-begotten of God stands by life's pathways and points us the way to her home in God. Later, Jews speaking Greek called her Sophia, the Wise Woman, a feminine personification of that essential attribute of omniscient God. In some poems she lives so triumphantly that she is imagined as the divine consort, the very woman of God.

But imaginations ran also in a second direction. To that original question, With what did God create the world?, came a second answer:

By the word of the LORD were the heavens made.
                                                                    (Psalm 33)

God spoke in Genesis: Let there be, and there was. Not God's sight, no divine agent, but the spoken word creates. And so there develops also a tradition about the divine word, the powerful word that calls into being that which it names, the word which creates reality by bringing order out of chaos. Throughout the Hebrew scriptures God is said to be speaking. God's word saves, condemns, blesses, destroys. It is God's word which the prophets speak, a burning coal on the lips, a sweet scroll to swallow.

In the last of the Old Testament books, the Book of Wisdom, Jews writing in Greek wed these two together: Sophia and Logos, wisdom and word, are interchangeably invoked as the names of God. God's wisdom, God's word—that is what we praise. The God who is wisdom and word is the God who knows us and by whom we are named. The way is set, the vocabulary prepared, the conceptual systems merged, so that two centuries later John's prologue can be written: In the beginning—the same story told again, anew—was the Word, the personified creation of God who created the world with God, Sophia become Christ, the powerful Hebrew speech made into Jesus. All things were made through him, John says of the Word.

Wisdom, Word: potholders for the sacred tripod. Wisdom, Word: God is personified by human attributes which are our pride—we, alone in the creation, like God, having wisdom, speaking words. Yet Paul writes that the wisdom of God is the opposite of ours: folly, foolishness, absurdity. And Mark suggests that the Word spoke most powerfully when he endured his passion in silence.

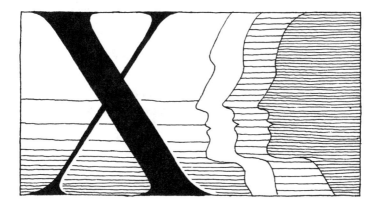

A *xat* is a totem pole, a sacred pillar which designates the center of the world by fixing on high the faces of the dead in a holy line between God and the people. The xat marks the journey with one's ancestors to God.

Late tradition says that St. Andrew, whom John names as the first disciple to follow Jesus, was martyred on an X-shaped cross, lifted up by ropes midway to God, leading us up to death.

Do merchants who choose the safe word Xmas realize that X is the first letter of the name of Christ? Christ was born to die, to lift us up to God. "And I, when I am lifted up from the earth, will draw the whole world to myself."

As we die we fix before us a sacred pole on which are Andrew and also Jesus, a xat which is a cross, an X cross. And that X is our journey to God.

For:

St. Andrew's X cross is Christ himself.
Our xat is Christ himself.
Our God is Christ himself.

Draw near to me and redeem me;
  because of my enemies deliver me.
They gave me gall to eat,
  and when I was thirsty, they gave me vinegar to
    drink.
As for me, I am afflicted and in pain;
  your help, O God, will lift me up on high.
                                          (Psalm 69)

Our yoke is our god—for whatever it is that we walk by, whoever it is who guides us, that is our god. The pattern we choose to follow, the frame we fit ourselves into, that is our god. We are not so liberated as we like to believe; most of us willingly don a yoke. It helps us walk the furrows without wandering aimlessly. It helps us plow our fields.

Best, then, if our God is our yoke. God's yoke, we say, is the easy wood, shaped differently from any regular ox-yoke, worn so thoroughly already by another that the wood is worn light. The saints who delighted to wear the yoke walked in the strangest directions, as if this yoke is one which takes old furrows away.

But furrows or not, a yoke binds together two burdened beasts. We share the toil, we breathe in concert and pull together. In binding us to one another, the yoke consoles. In joining us to Christ, the yoke saves. Indeed, with God as the yoke, we are coupled one to another by the very self of God.

Happy are they whose way is blameless,
who walk in the law of the LORD!

When your word goes forth it gives light;
  it gives understanding to the simple.
I open my mouth and pant;
  I long for your commandments.
Turn to me in mercy,
  as you always do to those who love your Name.
                                        (Psalm 119)

Beautiful and lofty, the joy of all the earth, is the hill
*   of Zion,*
*   the very center of the world and the city of the*
*   great King.*
Make a circuit of Zion;
walk round about her;
*   count the number of her towers.*
Consider well her bulwarks;
examine her strongholds,
*   that you may tell those who come after:*
"This God is our God for ever and ever."

                                         (Psalm 48)

Up, up the mountain they rise, Anna and Andrew, Miriam and
Monica. Blinded and burned by Uriel's fire, up they mount, up
the mountain of Zion. Bathed in the river, nursed by the cup,
surrounded by saints, blown to bits in the volcano, sailing
through the dark at the noon of the day, up to their Lord the
Queen. Come up, come down, children, to your Father. Come,
shepherd, and exult in the stronghold hidden in the skeletal
tree. What is that? A bird? A gemstone? A rock? Come up,

arise, ascend, you ill, you burdened, you enslaved. You need no wisdom, you need no words; the song soars before you. Up we leap; God will lead. Up, up the mountain of Zion, we rise to gaze at God.

> *Of Zion it shall be said, "Everyone was born in her."*
> *The singers and the dancers will say,*
>   *"All my fresh springs are in you."*
>   *(Psalm 87)*